SPARKLING DEW DROPS

RHYTHMIC PUBLISHERS

Contents

Rhythmic Publishers   *v*

Disclaimer   *vii*

Acknowledgements   *ix*

About the Book   *xi*

1. Festering Wounds   1

2. The Void   7

3. An Owl Named Jerome   9

4. Sharada's Marathon Run   16

5. A Comet   19

6. Who Is She?   25

7. Food For The Gods: The Ritual Of Human Sacrifice Among The Aztecs   29

8. Poems   35

9. Queer Queries   43

10. True Art   48

Author Biography

11. Mala Bhattacharya   59

12. Madhurima Roychowdhury   61

13. Debasri Mukherjee   63

14. Prakash Barai   65

15. Dr Debosree Ghosh   67

16. Shreshtha Chowdhury   69

17. Sanchita Chakraborty   71

18. Sayan Mukherjee   72

Rhythmic Publishers

-Seeking harmony through words.

We, at *Rhythmic Publishers*, believe in the power of words as a means of seeking harmony in a chaotic universe. We are eager to provide aspiring writers with a premium platform to express themselves. Attractive packages are available for both solo books and anthologies (editorial services and book design included). We work diligently to make a book the best version of itself and client satisfaction is our top priority.

Contact us on:

Instagram: @rhythmicpublishers

E-mail: rhythmicpublications23@gmail.com

We are also on **Twitter** and **LinkedIn**

Disclaimer

This anthology is a collection of poems, stories and write-ups written by talented writers from various parts of the country.

We have guided them not to use any copyrighted content and done our best to check plagiarism.

If any copyrighted content is detected, neither the publisher, nor the compiler nor the editor will be responsible in any way. Co-authors will be responsible for their own content.

All rights reserved. No part of this book may be reproduced, stored in a retrieval system, or transmitted, in any form by any means, electronic, mechanical, magnetic, optical, chemical, manual, photocopying, recording or otherwise, without the prior written consent of its Compiler.

Compiler and Editor: Aishi Bandyopadhyay

Book Layout and Cover Design: Romit Majumder

Acknowledgements

Rhythmic Publishers expresses its gratitude towards the extremely talented co-authors, who have enthusiastically contributed their write-ups for this book.

Sparkling Dew Drops is a collection of diverse literary works by talented authors across the country. Some are based on personal experiences and others are purely creative or factual. Each write-up in this anthology expresses distinctive emotions. Comprising of short stories, poems, prose and drama, this book is a unique imaginative ensemble which is bound to appeal to readers of all ages.

1

Festering Wounds

Mala Bhattacharya

The stubborn rain pounded on....... It was no longer coming down in sheets, nor with the force that it had shown in the early part of the evening. It had slowed down to a steady drizzle, interspersed with one or two blind pourings.

The wind accompanying it had long abated. Occasionally, a strong breeze stirred up the leaves of the tall roadside Banyan trees.

The glass-like droplets fell to the wet, dark tarmac of the road, where the remnants of the earlier rain water had made a shallow pool, reflecting the faint, shimmery lights of the distant vehicles, creating a mysterious haloed silhouette of the people walking, travelling slowly, seated in their cocooned cars.

Savitri stood there patiently under the canopy of the large Peepul tree, watching the rhythmic movements of life, completely in contrast to her agitated, beating, thumping heart.

She was almost soaked to the skin. The excuse of an umbrella held in her hand, remained exactly so! Her black bordered, dark pallu did cover her head, but the cotton had become soaked through and through, framing her round face. The twisted, knotted, tasselled fronds of the sari dripped droplets forlornly on her face.

Her features could not be ascertained, but as she slowly turned around facing the reflected lights of a busy city in the distance, one could see a mobile face. Wisps of peppered hair framed her forehead on both sides of her temple. The eyes had something special. Her look could hold the eyes of the onlooker for a few seconds more than was needed. A pair of rimless spectacles framed them. Completely sans make-up; - make-up at her age – ludicrous! She would have chortled up with amusement, crinkling up an aristocratic nose. She reminisced- while a half smile played on her lips;– her young son while playing with wheat flour, smeared handful of it on her face, all the while chuckling - "Aai look, your skin and flour have 'merged' into each other - no need for 'atta' dough - your checks can be rounded to make soft rotis !"

Suddenly - the smile of love turned into a grimace – in a flash she began to recall those terrible days of yester years. A hundred pound hammer began to pound at her temples bringing back those terrible days before her eyes. She swallowed, choking in her dry throat, trying desperately to push back those horrible, bitter thoughts and days, telling herself - 'No....... not today – No –No!'

She was startled out of her reverie, her nightmare –when a pair of piercing headlights of a speeding, hurtling car raced towards her. Instinctively, she jumped back a pace or two – but was unable to save herself from the huge mud splatter sprayed, not only across her sari, shoes and purse but even her spectacles were smeared with it partly. The car surprisingly stopped a little ahead. Through her mud-speckled glasses, she saw the chauffeur of the car sprinting towards her!

"Maaji–ghani khamma, maaf karo, I couldn't see the pothole till my front tyre dipped into it"– said the highly apologetic chauffeur.

"Maaji," gesturing to the car behind, "Saab bahut naarraj hain mujh par, aap please aiyay - aap se baat karna chahte hain; aur aap janha jaa rahin hain, woh aapko pounchanha denge – aap please mujhe maaf kijiye – please!"

Realizing that the brunt of the 'maalik's' anger would fall on the poor man, Savitri reluctantly followed the chauffeur towards the parked car at the side of the busy road.

Inside, once more, a deep, grave voice apologized and sincerely requested her to be seated inside the car, promising her that she would be dropped off safely to her destination.

As the roof-light was switched on for her easy, comfortable entry and settling down, she stole a glance at the suave, sober gentleman seated in the far corner of the seat. A surging pain hit her throat and heart, a pincer like grip seemed to choke her air off. She gave a muffled cough, gathering her wet pallu tightly across her mouth – almost gagging herself!

She forcibly calmed herself down, trying to concentrate on the almost one-sided conversation of him.

Turmoil raged through her mind and body. Every part of her being throbbed with the intensity of a guitar string. Still she managed to keep up her composure– till a red hot lava of anger shot through her belly, spewing up like magma– ready to flood her entire being.

With a swift movement, she opened her purse and found the razor-sharp, thin knife. Clutching it, she surreptitiously took it out in her right hand – she- she had been waiting -waiting –practising this scenario – playing it in her mind in a loop again and again for fifteen years.

Opportunity came.

The driver, probably a diabetic, asked Amit - yes, how could she even forget that brain - branded name- if he could stop the car to relieve himself? Amit nodded.

The driver swung to the left, found a suitable spot and braked. The rain, meanwhile had picked up again, falling in hazy slanting glass sheets. The driver soon disappeared behind the dense bushes.

Savitri sprang up! With a swift, dexterous move, she gripped the knife and plunged it straight into Amit's heart. Blood spewed out in a fountain-gush, smattering on everything - her specs, sari etc. The dark, oily, glistening, almost dark-chocolate-like blood spread slowly and began to pool.

Amit did give a piercing scream, but the noisy, relentless rain smothered it up. God was with Savitri that day, even if He wasn't during those terrible days! The passing cars were more intent on rushing home - dry and safe, rather than stopping to enquire about the expensive car 'stranded' on the road.

In a jiffy, Savitri was out of the car with ice-cold demeanour; she took the knife 'out' of Amit and washed away the blood. Then, with her wet pallu, she wiped clean her imprints as far as possible - the seat, the door handle. Well, the driver had seen her - she shrugged, it really didn't matter anymore! The deed was finally done and she found her spirits lifted up with a new found buoyancy and lightness.

Hurrying now, into the dark areas of the road – she simply disappeared – vanished, as if melting into the soft, chocolaty darkness.

The next morning, the completely composed, freshly bathed Savitri picked up the garden hoe, cleared the dead leaves, heaped them up and lit a fire. In it went the clothes that were witness to the scene - none noticed anything unusual. Of course the washed knife found its place among the other knives in the knife rack.

Over a warm cup of coffee, she switched on the telly, as was her wont to listen to the local news. Of course, the terrible murder of the philanthropist, Mr. Amit Anthony was being broadcast with necessary sobriety and regret.

Only a steely glint in her eyes betrayed the overwhelming emotion that had welled up as she had recalled those nightmarish days!

Amit and Baloo, her son, were as thick as thieves since their childhood. Baloo's father had succumbed to cancer early in life. Savitri, a young, utterly grief-stricken widow took solace in chanting the Sanskrit shlokas from the 'Bhagwad Geeta'. Pandit Shivkumar Shastry, the young, kind temple-priest often came home to correct and help Savitri's Sanskrit pronunciation. Who could have imagined, the young, innocent Amit had begun to plant seeds of doubt about the master-disciple relationship? His toxic thoughts soon overwhelmed simple Baloo – this Baloo, who had learnt to see, decipher the world through his mother's eyes! An ice-cold relationship began to develop between the two.

Soon it had to happen - and it happened. On a good bright spring morning, Baloo's lifeless body was fished out from the village well!

In the evening, sly Amit came to visit Savitri, a grief-stricken mother sitting quietly, mourning her beloved son's death, in the soft, lamp-lit room.

He hissed like a snake and with relish he said, "Aatya–I couldn't bear to see you both so close, especially, when my mother ran away to marry someone else, not caring to see what would happen to me! I just wanted to teach her a lesson through you!"

The foul smell of the burnt rexine, clothes and leaves finally broke into her reverie —

She got up slowly, suddenly feeling a thousand years old, yet, there was not an iota of remorse that clouded her mind. It was as if a great calm had descended upon her long, turmoil-filled life.

She had no qualms of dying or getting caught - In fact since yesterday - she felt shackle-free and unfettered!

No sooner had she gotten up, than, next door's Anil, a travelling ticket-checker called out.

"Auntie, where were you rushing off, yesterday night?

Your mud-splattered, blood smeared clothes seemed so unusual on you- you are always so clean - - - you looked at me, yet you turned away and disappeared into the dark!"

Savitri stood and listened, as if turned to stone – then feebly muttered - "Well - - - I seem to have fallen down at the meat market, I think .....!"

It really did not matter - the driver too..... Well,

..... 'Que Sera Sera ....!'

ppp

2
The Void

Madhurima Roychowdhury

Stumbling upon an obstacle,
I find myself in between crossroads.
I find an empty wheelchair with a buckle,
Worn and torn.

No life around,
All by myself.
Left to decide the right from the wrong.
Left to decide the black from the white.
Left to decipher the rainbow shades within.

Help hovers above the forest.
I try to wave a sign to seek help.
A ship sends out flares; in haste
The helicopter rushes off.
Alone, stranded, deserted.
I gaze at the vast emptiness.
It's all black and white but it's a farce designated.

SPARKLING DEW DROPS

The colours scream out in distress.
I can hear the muffled terror.
I creep in silence.
I walk on.

♡♡♡

3

An Owl Named Jerome

Debasri Mukherjee

I fly close to the ground. A ghostly shadow. Darker than the night! The graves below stand like silent sentinels, guarding the valley of death, where I seek a sign of life. I am quite proud of my visual acuity. Even among owls, I am quite the specimen. I can spot a mouse in the late evening from miles above. Many of my friends request my services when they fail to secure a catch for several nights on end. I like helping others. Maybe it comes from being an orphan growing up with an aging grandfather. My grandfather is wise. He used to be on the elders' council, meting out justice to digressers and solving problems for the community. Ever since I learned to fly, I have been accompanying him to these meetings; learning justice, learning the proper way to live.

A tiny flutter, a faint echo! All my senses are on high alert. I catch a whisper of a sound and search for the source. It is not evident. I decide to land. Maybe getting nearer the ground would help me find the source of the sound. Maybe, just maybe, I'll get lucky tonight. I land softly on a chipped and faded headstone. Like the memory of the person interred within. So much fuss over the event. All for naught. Memories are not slaves of custom! I sense a presence but see or hear nothing. A thrill of excitement runs down my back. Or is it fear? This is no mouse! It's close, very close. I look all around, yet see nothing, only the deepening shadows. Wait a moment! Deepening shadows?... It's passed midnight and dawn's quite some time away. There is no moon. The prospect of the shadows deepening at the current hour is ridiculous. I squint at the spot on the adjacent grave that had given me the illusion and jump back. The shadow is moving! Breathing fast, heart racing, I peer now at the faintly visible shape.

There is something odd about it. It doesn't seem solid; it's as if the surrounding darkness had tried to take a more corporeal form but didn't quite achieve it. My curiosity overwhelms fear. I hop a few paces nearer. This time I see the shadow turn its head and regard me; with equal interest, it seems. "You can see me." It's a statement, not a question. The voice that speaks is hoarse, soft, and raspy. A kind of voice I have never heard before. Another unfamiliar shiver runs down my spine. "Of course, I see you. I'm an owl!" I answer. "No other creature has been able to see me before now", the voice says. "That's because no other creature in these parts has eyes like mine." "You're pretty brash for an owl", says the shadow, seemingly amused. "Is it brashness to speak the truth?" I ask, "You stated yourself that no other creature has been able to see you before now". The shadow remains silent. I move a few more paces nearer. Any further and I'll fall off the headstone. "I wouldn't do that if I were you" the shadow figure speaks again. "Do what?" I ask. "Come any nearer." "Why?" "Well, I can't really tell you why since I'm not very sure of it myself. But I have a feeling that seeing me properly won't be very beneficial to your constitution."

I consider this statement while simultaneously attempting to discern the shadow's form. It seems human! Now I am flummoxed. I have never spoken to a human before and from whatever I've learned about these two-legged creatures from my grandfather and other elders, they are remarkably dull when it comes to instincts. They can hardly communicate effectively with each other, let alone other creatures. So, if the shadow creature is not human and not any other creature known to me, then what is it? Unless... "Are you a ghost?" I blurt out before I can properly consider the statement. The shadow, who seems to have lost interest in me, turns, and for the first time, gives me its full attention. "Why would you ask such a strange question?" it asks. "Because you're sitting in a dark graveyard. A shadow, yet not quite a shadow. You have the approximate shape of a human, yet you can speak to me. These are all very extenuating circumstances that make me consider the possibility that you may be an apparition, or in layman's terms, a ghost". I pause for breath and await its response. I can't explain it, but I am feeling very nervous about the answer. As if my entire life I have waited for a moment like this and have now reached it.

The silence stretches between us. Then, "I suppose I am a ghost", the shadow whispers in a tone of consideration, as if, it isn't very sure about the answer. "You seem unsure. Wouldn't you know if you were a ghost?" I ask. "Do owls have ghosts?" it queries suddenly. "Not that I'm aware of", I answer, surprised. I had never thought about that. I must ask my grandfather when I return. "Then how do you know about ghosts?" the shadow asks logically. "Well, my grandfather is a wise old owl. He has extensive knowledge about all creatures around us, especially about humans. He tells me about these things. He wants me to be one of the elders one day." "Why especially humans?" the shadow asks. "Because according to my grandfather, they are our greatest enemy. An enemy we cannot fight and so, must learn to avoid. He always says we should know our enemies better than our friends". There is a pause, then, "If I'm your enemy then what are you doing here talking to me?" I consider the question, then blurt out the obvious answer, "Well, technically you're not exactly a human. The best I can describe you is that you're a memory of a human. And memories can't harm you, can they?" "You know, that's probably the best explanation of a ghost that I have ever heard. No human could have given that. They are afraid of ghosts. Of memories." "Well, humans are afraid of a lot of things." I muse. "They seem to spend so much time being afraid that they completely miss out on the best things the universe has to offer. Or so says my grandfather." "I must meet your grandfather," the shadow states, "he seems too wise for his own good. Does he live in an oak?" "No. Why would you ask that?" I ask curious. "Well, we humans have this poem, 'a wise old owl lived in an oak, the more he saw the less he spoke...' and so on. I seem to have forgotten the rest. I seem to have forgotten a lot of things. But I do remember being a man", he says. "Well," I say, "my grandfather does speak less nowadays, but that doesn't seem to have anything to do with him living in an oak." A soft snort is all the response I get as the shadow lapses into silence again. There is something so intriguing about him, a sense of danger, a tug of the unknown, that I am transfixed.

I need to get back to my hunting. If I don't catch something nice and juicy tonight, it'll be another whole day before there is food in our nest. I don't mind so much, but my grandfather is weak and needs food. I know I should leave, yet I stay, staring across at the shadowy apparition. "I miss my phone", he says suddenly. "Phone? Is that the name of your mate?" I ask. I sense rather than hear his laughter. "So, you don't know everything about humans. A phone is a device that helps us talk to each other over long distances and learn more about the world. Though, recently it is becoming more and more the means for us to avoid talking to each other." "Well, why would you miss your phone if you're dead?" I ask. "Just because you're dead doesn't mean you are automatically rid of all the habits, good or bad, that you had grown into while you were alive." He answers with a touch of asperity. "I still miss my phone, my jukebox, and my car." I consider the choices for a moment. "You don't miss any of your people?" "Thankfully, no. I guess I'd had enough while I was alive". We stare at one another for a while, musing over the implications of his statement. Once again, I feel that strange shiver down my spine. Like a warning. Once again, I ignore it.

"Why did you land on that tomb?" he asks. "I thought I heard a mouse". He suddenly reaches down, I can't see where. He straightens and throws something over to me. Something big and squiggly and juicy. "There are many of those down there. I've been living with them. Go on. Catch it before it escapes." I look down at the creature. A sweet succulent mouse. It was already trying to sneak away. I sweep down and grab it with my talons. Hold tight. Open my beaks wide. Gobble it right up, wiggly tail and all. My, it's big. I can hardly breathe as I try to swallow the beast. As I'm struggling, I sense a movement. Even looking up is painful. Slowly I turn my head and freeze. The shadow is upon me. Sinister and threatening. His eyes. I stare at his eyes. They seem to burn right through me. He slowly extends his hands towards me. "I told you not to come nearer". The whisper is hardly audible. "If I can catch a rat, I can catch you. Nothing personal. You're just practice." He's towering over me. I can't move. I'm choking on my dinner. His shadowy fingers are closing around my tail. They are so cold. My entire body is frozen. I wish I could shut my eyes, but I can't. I must stare at the dark face as it comes inordinately closer and closer.

A snarl, a pair of red eyes, and another huge dark shape jumps right over me towards my captor. I feel him release my tail and slink away as the second shape advances on him. A blink and the first shadow is gone. The night seems lighter somehow. Warmer. Slowly I start feeling my body again. The second shadow had advanced a few paces following the first. Now it turns towards me, and I realize it's a dog. A huge black dog. Here is a definite tangible threat but somehow, I do not feel threatened. He just saved my life and I owe him. He saunters back looking at me quizzically. "What were you thinking getting down here? Didn't you know this place was haunted?" there's suppressed laughter in his tone, and I can feel my defences rising. Alright, I didn't know this graveyard was haunted. But then, who does? It's not like they have put up an advertisement. "What are you doing here if this is such a bad place to be?" I can hear the accusation in my tone. "I live here", he says. "What? How? Don't you get attacked?" "No. For some reason, they leave me alone." "Why did he try to hurt me?" I cannot help myself. I must know. "Who knows? It may be like he said. You were just practice. Anyways, I really don't have time to trade gossip with you now." He comes and stands near me. "You don't look capable of flying yet. Hop on." He crouches down on his haunches. "Thank you. I think I can." I try to spread my wings and take off. They won't open. "You can't. Now come on." There is no other option. This will be something for the record books. An owl riding a dog. Since there's nothing to do, I might as well enjoy the situation. I hop onto the dog's back, and he starts at a run. "Where do you live?" "My nest's too far for you to run. Just drop me off at the nearest tree." "All right. Here we go." He bounds forward into the night. I cling on for dear life.

I don't know how long we travel this way. But when he finally comes to a halt beside a tall and wizened banyan tree, the sky is getting darker. Dawn is near. I try my wings again and this time they unfurl, and I manage to fly up to the nearest branch. I look down to see the dog staring up at me. "Thank you!" I say. "I don't know why you helped me, but I am truly grateful. And I'm called Jerome." "You're welcome. Just don't tell anyone. Won't do my reputation any good if other dogs found out that I carried an owl on my back." He turns at that and starts to walk away. I call back one last time, "I won't tell anyone, but what is your name?" "Don't have any. Never did. But sometimes the humans call me Boy." He leaps forward and is soon lost to the night.

ᗡᗡᗡ

4
Sharada's Marathon Run

—♡—

Mala Bhattacharya

My friend who was all of 60; prepared herself for the
gruelling MUMBAI MARATHON and finally took part
in it. She
completed it too! This is her story through my eyes.
A steady pounding of feet
matched her pounding heart,
As she pushed on relentlessly, sweat
pooling on her sweat-shirt.
Each thump of her feet, drew
her close to her goal,
Doggedly she just thundered on,
no matter what the toll!
Morning after morning, she put
on her running shoes –
There was no looking back
no feeling the blues!

Before her snaked the white–striped asphalted road ;
One excruciating step followed by another,
Bent with fatigue, but not bowed.
She ran on preparing for the
great MUMBAI MARATHON
The dawn saw the day bright and crisp
A hint of cold, a bit of a nip
A sea of smiling faces, all eager to begin
And there she was with a huge happy grin!
The whistle blew and off they ran,
A happy medley of people to show
what they can
To run the big Mumbai Marathon!
Old soldiers, teachers, students galore,
All kinds of citizens rubbing shoulders as they run,
Athletes of renown and celebrities too,
all joined in the fun!
Past the high arched Bandra bridge
on and on she ran,
Drinking in the beauty of the
early morning sun.
The sea beneath looked calm and serene –
With gently bobbing boats; indeed a
picturesque scene!
She arrived now unto the sea-facing road;
Only to push her body to a
punishing mode
Sweat dribbled in rivulets, down
her tired spine,
With only one thought – 'I will complete –
this race is mine !'
Sharada, you did it girl,
quite commendably so,

We, your school-mates are justifiably
proud of you and more!
HURRAH! for your indomitable spirit;
And a big THANK YOU,
FOR WE ALSO RAN, IN SPIRIT
WITH YOU!!!

ᗡᗡᗡ

5

A Comet

Prakash Barai

Though whatever Mr Biswas is trying to convey in the tutorial class touches Aniket's ears, it can't go inside of it. His mind is busy making a world of fantasy of its own, where he is not alone; there is someone else there who is unaware of her existence in Aniket's world. The scenario was not like this even a few months ago. Knowingly or unknowingly, Aniket had always tried to keep a safe distance from the participants of the rat race. His scorecard for the 10th may reverberate it all. His parents are tired of repeating the same phrases to him again and again. However, Aniket is not displeased by all this, as his mere goal was to get promotion to the next class, and it is needless to say that he has achieved the distinction in that case.

At a quarter past six, B.B.Lane lights up. All the dedicated housewives finish their sweet and tangy gossip and go forward with their household chores. But they keep their keen eyes on this tutorial. Who comes with whom, what medium they use to come here, what kind of dresses they wear, especially the girls—everything is on the tip of their tongues. What would they do if Mr Biswas's class was not there? They probably would have found another area of interest.

It is the third class of Shakespeare's *The Tempest*. Mr Biswas always tries to give his best efforts to make all his students understand the true essence of literature. His strategies of comparing a complex text with a cartoon character or any movie's famous scene easily grab the students' attention. That's why he has been pretty popular among his students. Every year, his study room welcomes new inquisitive faces and bids good-bye to some familiar ones. As soon as the boards declare the results, parents start exchanging the numbers in search of a good tuition teacher, whose primary job is to teach the students, but to some extent also to make their kid understand the subject matter at first, then make them memorize it, and if possible, write their answer scripts in the exam so that they score well. After all, at the end of the day, they will brag about the marks among their friend circle. By the grace of God, Mr Biswas doesn't get these types of parents these days.

In this evening schedule, he has a boy of sixteen or seventeen, with soothing eyes, who looks naïve and clumsy, but has a distinguished look. Though the score card doesn't create an outstanding impact, Mr Biswas sees a spark in his eyes. The way he writes his views of an open ended question has given him a special place in the eyes of Mr. Biswas.

"And this is how Miranda got a first glance at Ferdinand, and you all know that the first glance is always very special," said Mr Biswas graciously.

As soon as he finished uttering his words, Aniket gets back to his senses. Now he can relate himself to the story.

He still remembers his first glance at Jaanvi. On the very first day, he was late for coaching, and as a punishment, he was standing by the door. Everyone was laughing timidly at him. But Jaanvi didn't laugh; rather, she looked at him with a sense of pity, as if she understood his embarrassment and he caught sight of her, sweat popping on his forehead. That glance at each other had a scintilla in it. That day, after going home, Aniket discovered a cloud of thoughts rumbling in his mind and it was quite clear that there was an urgency of rain. Aniket, unable to express his feelings to anyone else, took out his old friend from the wooden shelf and let the cloud shed, more or less in the form of an essay or a poem in blank verse. He found it difficult to put into words exactly how he felt. Days went by, and Aniket gradually got a permanent seat near Jaanvi. Whenever she is absent, Aniket gives her his notes with a sense of delight.

Mr. Biswas comes downstairs at 6 p.m. sharp. Sometimes, they come to the tutorial before six and discuss their hobbies, likes, dislikes, and so many other things. Jaanvi too was jubilant to get the company of Aniket. This boy seems to her to be an outlandish person who never does anything to show off. He just remains his true self. Otherwise, who would come with uncombed hair and a shirt torn from the armpit? In addition to that, he never asks about exchanging their numbers. He never even tries to impress her as the other classmates do in hundreds of possible ways. Maybe that was the reason that made them come closer.

Last week, due to some unavoidable circumstances, Mr. Biswas shifted his class to the early morning, instead of his regular time table. On that day, an astounding incident happened, possibly for the first time in Aniket's life. After dispersal from class, he was going his own way and nodding his head. A voice called him from behind.

"Aniket, is anyone going with you?"

"Nah! I am going alone as always with my rusty bicycle."

"Then would you mind if I asked you for a lift?"

Aniket wanted to utter 'yes, why not', but he was afraid that such a reaction would prove him a fool in her eyes.

"Why do you want a lift? You seem to be fine; you can walk. There are enough lights on the roads, and there are no dogs. Is there anything that you are afraid of?"

"Oh come on, Aniket! Don't be so stereotypical; it's not that a girl can only ask for a lift when she is in trouble!!"

"No, not at all. I didn't mean that," said Aniket. "Actually, in all my life, I didn't carry anyone on my bicycle, so I was perplexed and was in search of a perfect reply to your question."

"Oh! Now I get the point." Jaanvi said, "If you have no problem, then can we walk together up to that highroad?"

"Yes! Why would I have a problem?" he smiled.

For the first two to three minutes, they walked silently. Breaking the silence, Jaanvi said,

"Do you know which flower this is?"

"That's a Bougainvillea; who doesn't know it?"

"What a silly thing I said," murmured Jaanvi.

"Do you want some of the flowers in your braids, just like last Monday, when you applied a sunflower?"

"Wait a minute. That means you noticed...well, if you bring it, I wouldn't mind putting it in my braids," she continued, with crimsoned cheeks.

They soon came near the highroad, where their paths were separated, and both said, "See you on Monday."

It wasn't Prospero's magic that brought a tempest into Aniket's heart. At night, when all the city dwellers were busy relaxing their minds and bodies, Aniket went home, opened his diary and tore out two pages. He took up a pen and tried his best to give a proper form to his feelings. But what would he call it? An open letter, an open letter to his Miranda, the loveliest girl on earth. He dozed off after he was done writing it.

No, it's too late! When will she come? He gingerly looked into his shirt pocket; the letter was still there. He could have kept it inside his bag, but he wanted to keep his confession close to his heart.

It's half past six. Usually, she comes before six. What has happened today? Is she alright?

His restlessness is not overlooked by the keen eyes of Mr Biswas. At a certain point, he asks,

"Aniket, what happened? You seem to be lost somewhere!"

"No sir. I'm here."

"Then why do you glance at the door every two seconds? Are you looking for someone?"

"Sir, is Jaanvi ill today? Everyone is here; only she is absent. She generally never does this."

"Oh! Early in the morning, I got a call from her father. Her father has been transferred to their home town, and they left today, early in the afternoon. Didn't she tell you all?"

In the month of July, rain is very unpredictable. After a round of drizzle, one has to roll up his trousers to walk on B.B. Lane. Unlike everyone else, Aniket goes out of the tutorial, nodding his head as usual, and waits for everyone to leave. Then he goes on to take out his letter to Miranda. He takes a glance at it, tears it into a thousand pieces and throws it away. A bike coming at full speed from the opposite direction splashes dirty water on his white T-shirt. No one can see the glittering tears in the corner of his eyes.

Leaving a sigh, he looks vaguely at the sky. It is dark with a nimbostratus cloud.

ᗱᗱᗱ

6

Who is she?

Dr. Debosree Ghosh

At 8 PM, Ronit accepted his 8th trip request of the day. He called the passenger and confirmed the location as he always did. A woman's voice from the other side said, "Please come fast, I am waiting." Ronit reached the location and found a lady dressed in salwar kurti, who rushed into the cab, shared the OTP, sighed and leaned back.

Ronit noticed that the woman looked pretty in a blue salwar suit. She was as fresh as a rose. Though the temperature in Kolkata was between 40 to 43 degrees Celsius in the month of April, yet the lady looked absolutely fresh. Ronit thought she must have got out from an air conditioned place and hence was untouched by the heat of the city. He lowered the temperature of the AC in his cab. He was playing his favourite song and driving smoothly. After the hot day, the evening felt soothing and comfortable. The destination was a place in Salt Lake. After some 20 minutes, Ronit noticed that the lady was absolutely silent. He thought that she must have fallen asleep. He lowered the volume of the song and concentrated on his driving.

He reached the destination at 9:40 PM, ended the trip and turned back to notify his beautiful passenger. To his utter surprise, he noticed that the lady was almost reclined on the seat and that her eyes were closed. He called out but there came no response. So he got down and went over to the back seat. His heart skipped a beat as he noticed that the lady was cold and had no pulse. Ronit was perplexed. He hurriedly sprinkled some water on her face but nothing happened. He hastily returned to the driver's seat, started the car and headed for the nearest hospital.

In the meantime, he heard a strange sound from the back seat. A strange voice said, "Please help." Ronit stopped the car and turned back once again, only to get the shock of his life! The beautiful lady was sitting up, her eyes were blinking and she was speaking in a strange, trembling voice, "Help me! I am in emergency." She was pointing to the charging point in the car. Ronit didn't understand anything and couldn't believe his eyes. He somehow gathered all his strength and asked, "What?"

The lady said, "Please put this in the charging point." Her voice was shrill and it sounded different this time. Ronit saw that she was holding something in her hands. He thought that it was her phone. He asked, " How?"

"With this," she said and handed over a strange wire to Ronit. It was a charger, Ronit understood. He had parked the car on the roadside. "Hurry up, the battery will die again, please," said the lady, in a strange voice. Ronit put the jack into the charging point in the car. The lady's eyes brimmed up, her beautiful lips parted with a broad smile. "Thank you so much. Now drop me at my destination please. I will pay extra. It's urgent. I need help. Please," she said. Ronit was dumbfounded. He was still in shock. He didn't understand how the lady who had no pulse a few minutes ago and was dead cold suddenly sat up! What was so serious that she needed help at this hour! What was she going to the destination for! It was not a hospital. It was the address of a multinational information technology company. Yes, these companies work day and night in shifts. Ronit thought that she must be an employee there.

After 5 minutes, the lady said in her sweet, normal voice, "I do not have words to express my gratitude. You saved me. I would have been dead otherwise." Ronit didn't understand and said, "I do not understand Madam. Are you unwell?"

The lady smiled and said, "I never fall sick."

Ronit didn't understand.

"I just need some help and then I will be fine."

Ronit reached the destination, stopped the car and told her her fare. The lady said, "Please unplug the wire now."

Ronit removed the charger from the charging point and turned around to give it back to her. The lady paid the fare and got down. Ronit had lots of questions that he wanted to ask her, like, when he had checked her pulse, why was her wrist as cold as ice? Now, while giving the charger back, his hand touched her and he found that she was warm.

Ronit got down from the car and shouted out to the lady who had started walking down the ramp towards the main gate of the office. "Madam, please stop." The lady stopped and looked back at him. Ronit came running and asked, "Who are you?"

She smiled and said, "Hi, I am Lima, I am a humanoid, a little different and a lot similar to you humans. I am a human-like creature created by the merging of robotics, human computer interface, brain mapping and digital legacy, powered by artificial intelligence. I have been transferred the memory of the wife of a man who owns me and maintains me. His human wife expired. He is out of station and my system has been hacked. It has got a bug in it, it seems. I am losing charge fast, very fast. I am running in safe mode. I need immediate help and so I am here."

Ronit couldn't believe what he had just heard. She looked like a normal woman. She was beautiful and had make-up on. Her beautiful face, eyes and lips, all bore human expressions. He couldn't believe that she was indeed a humanoid and not a human! Lima broke the silence, "When his wife expired, the man stored her memory and transferred it all to me. I have been trained with all her feelings, expressions, reactions, intelligence and emotions. I have been trained with her voice and her qualities, abilities and disabilities. I do all household works, go shopping, look after the accounts of his business and can satisfy all his needs. I am Lima, wife of Mr. Hirak Mukherjee." Suddenly her voice changed and she was blinking.

Ronit understood everything now. He said, "Got it Madam. You need help. Let's go inside." They went in to fix the bug in the system.

We are soon going to be living in a world full of our
loved ones who will be humanoids and we will be the
humans. Bugs and hacks will have to be taken care of in all
our lives. Humanoids need humans to fix the bugs. Thus,
AI can probably never overpower human intelligence.

ᐅᐅᐅ

7

Food for the Gods: The Ritual of Human Sacrifice among the Aztecs

Shreshtha Chowdhury

Cannibalism is mostly considered a taboo in Western culture, with the exceptions of the sacraments in Christianity. Accounts of cannibalism can be found throughout the history of the world which include instances of cannibalism of the Aztecs. The Aztecs and the Maya people make up a violent part of Mexico's history. The Aztecs were originally a nomadic tribe known as the Nahua. George C. Vaillant in *Aztecs of Mexico: Origin, Rise and Fall of the Aztec Nation* writes "... the Tenochcas, the Mexico City Aztecs, began wandering in A.D. 1168". The rationale for Aztec human sacrifice was purely a matter of survival. According to Aztec cosmology, the Sun God Huitzilopochtli was waging a constant war against darkness, therefore the Aztecs had to feed the Sun God with human hearts and blood to get their lives preserved. Sir James Frazer in *Le Rameau d'Or* (vol. 4), found out that this sacrifice is a "means of perpetuating the divine energies" that is "to revivify the Gods by establishing a link with the deities", more prominently they hold the Sun as the source of all energy which needs feeding with lives. The ritual of human sacrifice had another purpose in expanding the Aztec empire. The large-scale display of skulls was considered a reminder of the empire's strength and the extent of its dominion. Anthropology professor John Verano stated that it was a tremendous honour for many captured soldiers, slaves and Aztec citizens to sacrifice their hearts for a blessed afterlife willingly. Dave Roos in *Human Sacrifice: Why the Aztecs Practiced This Gory Ritual*, wrote that the Aztecs also practised a form of ritual cannibalism. The victims' bodies after being relieved of their heads were gifted to noblemen and other community members.

Research continues to reveal details about this civilisation. In Belize cave and Chichen Itza, multiple skeletons of children have been found that show evidence of human sacrifice. An article suggested that Diego de Landa, a priest and a bishop, shared insights into the rituals among the Maya that included human sacrifice "... they gathered and made a pierced hole through the member, across from side to side and passed a quantity of cord, they [also] anointed the statue of the demon with the collected blood." Records showed that the dynasty of Cocom or Cocomes was part of the Maya family, who controlled the Yucatan Peninsula. Between 1566 and 1579, the Mayas practised cutting off the heads of the lords of Cocoms when they died and used to clean the flesh from their skulls and then saw off half the crown on the back leaving the jaws and the teeth. This practice of mutilation of bodies, according to them, were human trophies, which were kept for all faithful to pray to. Human sacrifice significantly increased among the Mayans in the Terminal Classic and Post-Classic Periods.

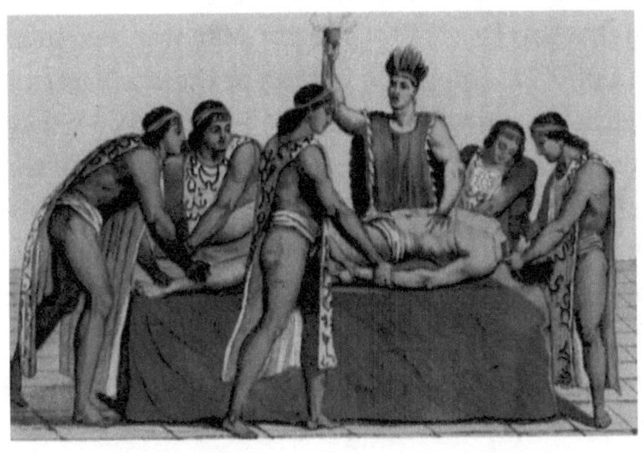

Linda Schele, in an article named *Ritual Human Sacrifice*, describes the death by projectiles in which the victims were painted blue, tied to a post, stretched across a stone altar and then their hearts were excised. The heart was elevated as a special offering to the Sun God, and the corpse was rolled down the pyramid. The Aztecs sacrificed slaves (most of them were war captives) and even their children. The ideology of Aztec human sacrifice stated that the victim's heart nourished the Gods. Claud Levi-Strauss in *Tristes Tropiques*, depicted that the Aztecs had a "maniacal obsession with blood and torture". Marvin Harris in *Cannibals and Kings* (1977), shared details regarding this sacrifice, where he stated that after the heart was elevated and offered, the corpse was butchered with its limbs for human consumption. They send the torso to feed the animals.

Another important Aztec ritual was the Feast of the Flaying Men. During this ritual, men were flayed and later their flesh was eaten. During this Feast, more than a thousand captives from Yancuitlan were sacrificed. David Carrasco in *Cosmic Jaws: We Eat the Gods and Gods Eat Us*, stated that this Feast of the Flaying Men was held in honour of the God Xipe Totec. The victims or the war captives were dressed as the living image of Xipe Totec and then they were sacrificed. After the sacrifice, they were flayed and the men put on the skin. After twenty days the skins were taken off and buried. The victims' body was cut up and one of the thighs was given to the king, it was then eaten in a bowl of dried maize stew.

Women were also used as victims in Aztec rituals. A woman was selected to represent the Mother Goddess in the harvest festival. This woman was decapitated and flayed and a young man wore her skin. The skin from one of the thighs was removed and was worn as a mask by the high priest who served Centeotl, the maize Goddess. For the Feast of the goddess Toci, a woman was chosen. Fray Diego Duran in *Book of the Gods and Rites and the Ancient Calendar*, mentioned that the priest beheaded this woman in a way so that the priest was drenched from head to foot in blood.

The festival of the God of Fire was the climax of the entire Aztec year. Newlywed couples were chosen as victims. They wore ceremonial robes associated with the fire god. Then they were thrown into the flames of the fire gods' altar, and were raked out of the fire by the attendants of the high priest and their hearts were torn out. Another major festival of the Aztec calendar was an offering to the rain God, where children were drowned. There was the Feast of Xipe Totec (God of spring and renewal of nature), where victims were pelted with arrows so that their blood fell like rain. Then they were flayed and the skins were dyed yellow. The priests then wore the skins as a symbol of how the earth wore its new mantle at the end of the rainy season.

A cinematic version of this human sacrifice of the Mayan civilization has been explored by director Mel Gibson in his film *Apocalypto* (2006). The film excels with its art, architecture and setting of different epochs and regions within the Mayan civilization. Mel Gibson's historical action-adventure film *Apocalypto* (2006)shows Jaguar Paw (Rudy Youngblood), a member of an Edenic tribe, who was captivated and marched to a Mayan metropolis to be sacrificed to the Gods. The film has a spectacular human sacrifice scene, in which the slaves line up on the side of a gigantic pyramid, where crowds surround them. Gibson meticulously prepares the audience for the scene, where the hearts of the slaves are ripped out of chests and their heads lopped off and tossed down the steps to the cheering crowd to appease the angry Gods, who were spoiling their crops. Without sacrificial nourishment, the universe would fall apart. Sharing a meal with God created a communal bond. The ceremony in the film is very faithful to the most lurid sources of the Aztec rituals. In this film, a scene of Eclipse sets off a major change and deadly series of events during the human sacrifice scene. In one of the pivotal scenes of the film, the main character, Jaguar Paw, is about to be sacrificed in a Mayan altar but is spared when the moon suddenly obscures the Sun. The Mayans take the eclipse as a sign that the Gods have been appeased, so his life is ultimately pardoned. The historical accuracy of the portrayal of the priests in the film is subjected to artistic interpretation. Religious and spiritual leaders held significant power and influence over their followers by claiming to possess supernatural knowledge or abilities. A still from Gibson's Apocalypto portrays Mayan culture through their violent, bloodthirsty rituals (below), the slash of a knife into the flesh and the still-beating heart of a human victim held up to a gaping sky.

Evidence of human sacrifice in ancient culture is often fragmented. Mesoamerican writings and artwork that had been unearthed needed to be combined with archaeology, forensics, and bones excavated from burial sites for a more thorough understanding of the underlying reasons and methods of these rituals. Ruling elites were often the ones who decided who was to be sacrificed, and for what purpose. Most of these ceremonies were public, tainted by an undercurrent of power and intimidation running through the veins of the elites.

ᘖᘖᘖ

8
Poems

Debasri Mukherjee

I

The Road That Never Was

My road is of mud and stone,
Red and brown, sad, and worn.
Shifting seasons, drought, or rain,
My road is a river of strife and strain.

My road is a truant, a nomadic call,
Come, O ye traveler, come ye all!
My road is a menagerie, a roving circus show,
With reptiles and birds and mammals in tow.

My road is angry, my road is fierce,
It blogs me down with passion and tears.

My road is a trial of spirit and will,
Of wandering feet and minds never still.

My road leads on from my door to more,
And I must follow for glory and lore.

❧❧❧

II

Eyes Wide Open

Life is easy with eyes closed!
But is it worthy when we don't behold?
I walk'd the frequent paths a'fore
Deaf to the songs of joy and sorrow.
Blind to the myriad smiles and tears,
The crossplay of life flowing through the years.

The ancient delinquent on the pavement floor,
Whiling away time for evermore.
The sprouting young lives, careless and free,
Trailing life on a kite's tail, racing the wind with glee.
The lovers' tiff, the mother's scold,
The shy young girl, the puppy learning to be bold,
The high and mighty treading stiff and straight,
The woman hoity toity antsy with the wait.

The dirty little urchin dancing in the rain,
The resigned farmer gathering his grain.
The grumpy opulent, hailing a cab,
The youth broke and merry, smoking on a tab.
The naïve servant girl tattling with ease,
The loyal old retainer refusing to please.

The rotund matriarch shopping for the fest,
The kempt office worker hurrying without haste.
And amidst the chaos, pink flowers from a ledge,
The azure blue sky peeking over the edge.
Nostalgic sweet memories come to mind,

Still moments in the humdrum of life.
I walk through them as they pass through me,
These are but the fleeting memories to see.

Eyes wide open, I look, and I behold,
Because what's the point in living, with eyes closed?

ᗡᗡᗡ

III

What If?

What if there were no homes, only open fields ahead?
The sky above, and the earth beneath our tread.
What if no one cared for things anymore?
The rocks were our hearth and the trees our door,
What if nothing could hold us from going anywhere?
Only the stride of our feet, and the distance from here
to there.
What if we had no money, nor any possessions to keep?
Food was a'plenty and the rivers clean and deep.
What if every day, we lived like it was our last?
Then the dream may come true, amidst nature infinite
and vast.

 PPP

IV

Music of Life

I can hear the music play!
The Azaan's tune deep in my dreams,
The music is without, it is within.
The early morning song of birds,
The music rushes in, eager to be heard.
The whisper of leaves in the morning breeze,
The music is in my heart, waiting for release.
The silence of the midday sun,
It's just a pause, before the tune returns.
And dusk brings the waning notes,
I hear them sing the farewell ode.
To the day well done, the rhythm fading away,
The night queen reigns, and yet I hear the music play!

V

The Last Bond

The little bird flew high in the air,
Its strong wings fluttering with glee,
At last, after endless days and nights,
It has had its chance to flee!
The golden cage, so carefully kept,
Its bars so pretty yet so strong.
The little bird called all night while the world slept,
Unperturbed by its mournful song.

Then came the little girl who cried,
At the little bird's plight to see,
She begged one and all to let it go,
But they were deaf to her entreaties.
Then one early morn she came,
Stealthily up to the gilded cage,
And opened the precious glittering door,
Defying her elders' might and rage.

And thus, it was how the little bird,
At last had its chance to flee,
Breaking all human bonds but one,
That had set it free.

᠌᠌ᗆᗆᗆ

VI

Independence Day

Moonlight bathes the snowy peaks of Dras,
A rare tranquil silence abounds.
Heaven and earth are in harmony for once,
The night is still but for a lone wolf howl.
The sound of the blast is a siren call,
A broken note in a maestro's stroke.
The moonlight shatters with the burning glow,
And peace lies tattered amidst the heavenly abode.
Dawn bathes the valley in a crimson light,
A familiar sight of carnage reigns.
The serene tranquility still abounds,
But now the silence is that of the grave.
Amidst the dead walks a child,
A pale shadow of life in a land of death,
She searches for her mother amongst the carnage
And finds, the shredded tricolor instead.
The nation is alive with fervor and joy,
Celebrating yet another Independence Day,
And far away beneath the snowy peaks of Dras,
A child cries for her mother to take her away.
From the frigid and harsh loveless land,
The torn tricolor in one small hand,
She picks her way through the horror of the day,
Bound forever with terror and fray.

ᴘᴘᴘ

9
Queer Queries

❦

Sanchita Chakraborty

"After Cinderella leaves the ball in haste and loses one of her glass slippers, the prince is determined to find the owner of the slipper. He sends out a proclamation that he will marry the woman whose foot fits the slipper. The slipper is taken around the kingdom, and despite many attempts, it fits no one until it reaches Cinderella's house.

Cinderella's stepsisters try on the slipper, but it doesn't fit them. Cinderella, who has been hidden away, asks to try it on. Despite the mocking and disbelief of her stepsisters, the slipper fits her perfectly. She then produces the matching slipper from her pocket, proving she is the mysterious beauty from the ball.

The prince marries Cinderella, and she forgives her stepsisters for their previous mistreatment. Cinderella and the prince live happily ever after."

Maa enters with a phone.

Maa: Diya, you are 26, what a perfect time to read "Cinderella"!

Diya: Maa, there is nothing called perfect time. The very term 'perfect' leads to the rejection of the 'real'. And I think…

Maa: Uff! Stop being philosophical all the time. Take your phone, it was in the hall. Nandini called you twice.

Diya: Okay, thanks; now let me enjoy my 'me time.'

Maa: Yes, 'me time', a new term that creates distance within a family, and your 'me time' is nothing but overthinking, right?

Diya: I never realized the extent of my influence. I'm making you thoughtful…

Maa: Unbearable!

Maa leaves the room.

Phone rings… 'Where are you now?

Atlantis, under the sea, under the sea

Where are you now? Another dream

The monster's running wild inside of me,

I'm faded, I'm faded… …'

Nandini picks up the phone.

Diya: Sorry darling, my bad. The phone was in the hall.

Nandini: Apology accepted. Now tell me what are you doing?

Diya: Now I'm just wasting time by talking to you. Before that, I was reading "Cinderella".

Nandini: Nice. Pardon, what?

Diya: Yes! "Cinderella".

Nandini: So, is there any new update on Prince Charming?

Diya: Stop mothering me.

Nandini: No, no, tell me. What happened to that boy?

Diya: First of all, he's not a boy, but a man. Secondly, I don't prefer to stalk people I don't like. And finally, he is not at all 'my Prince Charming', so I don't want to think about him.

Nandini: Oh! So what are the qualities you want in 'your man'?

Diya: Nandu, you know I don't like these things, I don't like to commodify a person. He just needs to be a good human being with whom I can connect well, and that's all.

Nandini: But...

Diya: Let's not talk about this. Tell me, are you going to attend tomorrow's party?

Nandini: I detest this type of party. So I haven't decided yet. Let's see what His wish is!

Diya: 'His wish'... ummm hmmm...

Nandini: Yes, I purely believe that everything depends on His wish. Don't you think we are just puppets, playing the roles that He has scripted?

Diya: Yes, I also believe that everything is predestined. But the other day I was listening to a podcast on the 'Copernican Principal' and they were saying, "Stop thinking of yourself that special, you are nothing but an ordinary man. You are just one species on a small planet in a vast universe", and to some extent, I find it beneficial. Because it transforms my fatalistic worldview into a providential one. Now I can think that the benevolent higher power is directing my actions toward a meaningful purpose.

Nandini: Yes, Providentialism truly empowers us. Maybe Frances Hodgson Burnett refers to this 'benevolent higher power' as 'magic' when she says, "Everything is made out of magic. Leaves and trees, flowers and birds, and foxes and squirrels and people". But the podcast is also somewhat true. We are ordinary; but not unimportant.

Diya: Wow, 'ordinary but not unimportant', antithesis. So what do you think we are?

Nandini: Ahhh! That's an awesome question. Sometimes I think we should start a talk show to make the universe know that we are not at all ordinary, that there is an 'extra' before the word.

Diya: Yeah, we should. We are exceptional people who can talk sensible nonsense!

Nandini and Diya laugh together.

Diya: See, that matrimonial advertisement "tall, fair, pretty, well educated" can't define me. Because we know, "Beauty lies in the eyes of the beholder", so no one can be categorized as 'beautiful', and if now anyone asks me about the periodic table, he can understand that I'm not well educated! I can only say that I'm a pure soul.

Nandini: Yes, I was expecting this type of answer from you. But that is a spiritual perspective. We're souls in the eyes of the Divine. But have you ever thought what makes you you?

Diya: Maybe my actions, thoughts, values, and beliefs create a unique self. And I think Hindu Philosophy calls this the 'samskaras'.

Nandini: Samskaras are very powerful. The Bhagavad Gita describes how actions and samskaras affect the soul's journey through multiple lifetimes.

Diya: Oh, yes, you were reading the Bhagavad Gita in the last vacation. So does "Gita" believe in reincarnation?

Nandini: Yes, obviously. In one of the chapters it states, "As a person puts on new garments, giving up old ones, the soul similarly accepts new material bodies, giving up the old and useless ones".

Diya: Wow. And as far as I know, not only Hinduism, but Jainism, Buddhism, Sikhism, ancient Egyptian religions and early Christianity also support this concept.

Nandini: But sometimes I wonder, if the soul is eternal, how will one get salvation?

Diya: Just like the soul and its journey, different religions have varying views on salvation. Whether salvation means liberation from the cycle of birth and rebirth or union with God, I believe one can attain it with devotion, faith, knowledge and righteous living. And if we're not getting salvation at the present moment, we can live happily and have a perfect life.

Maa enters.

Maa: Let me see, who is she? Weren't you telling me just half an hour before, "There is nothing called perfect, perfect is just the rejection of the real"? Now what's happened to you?

Put the call on speaker.

Dearies, I'm glad that you, in your mid-twenties, are thinking about these things. But don't overthink. You lack the experience to critically assess these complex concepts. And always remember, both spiritual exploration in isolation and social interactions are equally important. Okay?

Nandini, go and have your dinner, your mother must be waiting for you. Diya come fast.

Silence for a few seconds.

Nandini: No more today. Good night.

Diya: Yes, bye. Good night.

ᐅᐅᐅ

10
True Art

Sayan Mukherjee

"Wonderful! This is my first time at an art exhibition. Isn't this amazing David?" said Antonio, very excited.

"This is the biggest art exhibition in all of America. The Summer Art Festival, Texas. It is truly magnificent. And by the way, do not call me David. Use my undercover name Tim, Mathew. Are you forgetting that we are on duty right now? We are here to check upon Pablo Giordano. A very dangerous and psychotic serial killer who has committed many unspeakable crimes. He started killing when he was just fourteen. His first victims were his mother and his step father, whom he killed because they didn't agree to buy him new toys. Since then, he has killed twenty seven different people-some of his friends, cousins, relatives and neighbours are on that list. Can you imagine that? However, he was released on probation after serving thirty five years in prison. Since then, he has changed. He has become a painter and earns his bread by selling his paintings. So save your excitement for later," said David.

"Okay! Okay! I get it. But what kind of a name is this – Mathew. I'm Italian. Can't the director of FBI give me a more meaningful name? Huh!" said Antonio, quite disappointed.

It has been three years since our hero, Antonio, has saved the world. He now lives in Texas, where he was gifted a bungalow and a convenience store by The President himself. He completed his graduation from a college in Texas. He is also a trainee in the FBI Academy under David Jones.

As they went down the hallway, they could see many different paintings by many different painters. But there was one painting which caught Antonio's attention. It was not an extraordinary one, but it had something which made it interesting – a beautifully painted scenery of a lake with hills in the background. And the foreground was covered with lush green bushes. A close examination revealed a gravestone peeping out through the bushes in the foreground, and this was what made the painting stand out from the others. Antonio and David stood in front of the painting, gazing at the intricate details of the masterpiece.

"Isn't this an extraordinary one?" said a man tapping on Antonio's shoulder from behind.

Antonio turned around and noticed a tall and handsome man looking at him. He was more than six-feet tall with a well-built body and was probably wearing the costliest suit among all the people present in the hall.

"Indeed it is," said Antonio. "And who are you?"

"My name is Pablo Giordano and I am the creator of this masterpiece," said the man.

"What?" Antonio said to himself, "So this is the serial killer David was talking about. He sure doesn't look like one."

"What happened young man? Are you getting frightened? You do not have to be afraid of me. Sure, there was a time when people were, but now I am friend to everyone," said Pablo in the calmest voice. "May I ask what your name is?"

"It's Mathew," Antonio replied.

"And who is this nice man you have come with?" asked Pablo again.

David, who was quiet this whole time, said, "I am Tim Harper, a journalist for *The Texas Times* newspaper. This is Mathew Wade, my personal assistant. We have come to write about this art exhibition."

"Very good," said Pablo. Just as he turned around to go the other way, a waiter who was carrying lemon soda on a serving tray collided with Pablo and the soda spilled on Pablo's expensive suit. The waiter quickly pulled out a towel and tried to soak the liquid, but Pablo made a gesture with his hands and told the waiter that it's okay.

"I am extremely sorry Sir. I should've..."

"It's okay. What is your name?" said Pablo in a firm voice.

"It's Jeremy, Sir," the waiter replied.

"Well Jeremy, be more careful next time," said Pablo, with a smile on his face. He then went the other way.

Shortly after, the sound of an alarm was heard throughout the building, which indicated that the auction was about to begin in the main hall. Everybody, including Antonio and David, went towards the main hall.

Entering, they saw a huge room, dimly lit with a stage opposite to the door. The whole room was heavily guarded by men wearing black suits and black sunglasses. There were many circular tables. Each table had three chairs. They saw Pablo sitting in a chair, waving at them. Pablo was wearing a different suit now.

"Come here. I have kept seats for you two," said Pablo to Antonio and David.

"Thank you very much Pablo," said Antonio, sitting down.

"Is this your first time at an auction, young man?" asked Pablo.

"Yes."

"So sit tight because the temperature is about to get hot," said Pablo again.

With the ring of a bell the auction started. The auctioneer stood behind a podium placed to the left of the stage. There were twenty different paintings listed for the auction that day. With every bid, the auctioneer shouted 'SOLD' – each time his voice was filled with enthusiasm. After nineteen different paintings came Pablo's painting. After a tough battle, it was bought by a rich Spanish couple for five million dollars. The auction ended with the ring of a bell.

After the auction, a grand lunch was organised in the lawn. There were hundreds of items on the menu – Italian, Mexican, Continental, Chinese, Indian and many more.

"Hi there, Mathew and Tim. Did you guys write about today's event?" asked Pablo.

"Yeah, Yeah. It is surely going to be one of the headlines in tomorrow's newspaper," answered Antonio.

"Don't worry about that Pablo. We are *The Texas Times'* finest," said David.

"Thank you Tim."

"Well Pablo, can I ask you a question?" asked David.

"Sure Tim," answered Pablo.

"Can we interview you tonight? About what led you to become a painter? Maybe you can show us more of your paintings."

"NO. I mean, I am kind of busy tonight. Here, you can take my card. Call me next week. If I'm free, I'll let you know," said Pablo, his voice trembling slightly. He quickly pulled out a handkerchief and started wiping his face. "Excuse me, I have some work to do at home. I should get going," he said and started walking towards the parking lot.

"Did you notice something strange in his behaviour Mathew?" said David smiling. "Let's follow him."

"There is definitely something fishy,"said Antonio.

They quickly followed Pablo to the parking lot. Pablo seemed very cautious. He was constantly looking behind him to check whether he was being followed. He got in his car and sped from the scene. Antonio and David noticed that it was a black Rolls Royce.

"He sure is rich," said Antonio.

David pulled out a walkie talkie from his side bag, adjusted the frequency and said, "This is David Jones requesting for back up ASAP. The suspect is in a black Rolls Royce leaving the Summer Art Festival. Follow the car maintaining a distance, and do not engage. I repeat, DO NOT ENGAGE."

"Copy that, David. We're on our way," said a voice from the other end.

David said, "Come on Antonio, let's follow him."

They quickly got into their car and started off behind the Rolls Royce.

After about an hour or two, Pablo's car came to a stop. Pablo got out and opened the massive doors of his mansion and drove his car inside. By that time, the other FBI agents had also arrived at the scene.

David turned on his walkie. "The suspect has entered the house. Park your car around the corner and wait there until further instruction," he said.

"Roger that, David," said a man.

Antonio said, "Wait? Can't we bust in right now?"

"Do you have any evidence against him, Antonio? If you want to be an agent you have to be patient."

"Okay David," said Antonio, sounding bored. He switched on his mobile and started playing games.

After an hour or two, Pablo's car left the house. David ordered everybody to follow the car.

ppp

TWO HOURS EARLIER

Pablo entered the house, locked his door, switched on the door alarms and went to take a shower. After that, he made himself a cup of coffee and sat on the sofa, holding the TV remote. Just as he was about to switch on the TV, he heard the sound of a voice coming from the room to his left.

"Let me go, you moron. You can't get away with this," said a man, in a shaking voice.

Pablo put down his cup and went into the room. "So you have come back from unconsciousness, huh? Now I need to tie up your mouth too," he said.

Pablo went across the room in search of a duct tape. In the middle of the room, sat a man in a chair, his legs tied up, his hands nailed to the armrests, blood dripping down the chair. It was Jeremy, the waiter.

"What do you want? What did I do to you?" asked Jeremy, crying.

"Did I ask for anything? I just want you to realise what you did to me," Pablo said.

"Is this about the time I spilled the drinks on you?"

"Tell me Jeremy, when you were a child, how did your mother make you realise your mistakes?"

"She never scolded me. She just talked me through it..."

"Don't worry Jeremy, I will make you understand that there are consequences for one's actions. Those who make mistakes must face punishments," said Pablo, in a calm voice, grabbing a kitchen knife from one of the drawers.

Suddenly, the telephone rang.

"Be quiet," said Pablo to Jeremy. He picked up the phone and waited for the caller to speak first.

"Hello, may I speak to Mr. Pablo?" a voice said.

"Hello. I am Pablo Giordano. And who do I have the pleasure of speaking to?" asked Pablo.

"Hello, Mr. Pablo. This is Tim Harper speaking. Remember me, we met at the art exhibition. Well, can we interview you tonight?" said David.

"I said to call me next week, didn't I? I'm busy now. I'll call you..."

"HELP! HELP ME PLEASE!" Jeremy begged, hoping to get a response.

Pablo hung up the phone immediately. "You have become quite a pain for me Jeremy. It is high time I give you what you deserve," said Pablo, as he slit Jeremy's throat slowly. Jeremy gagged for some time because of the blood entering his windpipe. After about two minutes, he died, his eyes open, his clothes soaked in blood.

Pablo brought out a big garbage bag and put Jeremy's body inside it. He tied the bag with a rope and placed the bag in the trunk of his car. Then he cleaned his entire house so that no trace of blood could be found. After that he took a shower and cleaned himself thoroughly. Then he put a shovel, his Glock 18, his drawing kit and a canvas inside his car.

After that, he lit a cigarette and drove the car into the woods.

ᐳᐳᐳ

FOUR HOURS LATER

David was following Pablo's car maintaining a safe distance. He had predicted that Pablo might take the road that led to Sam Houston National Forest.

"Warn all our units at Sam Houston National Forest, Antonio. We will search his car there," said David.

Antonio switched on his walkie. "This is Antonio Rossi, requesting all units at the Sam Houston National Forest to track and follow a possible suspect driving a black Rolls Royce. The suspect could be armed so keep your guard on. You are to follow the car until further instructions."

"Roger that. This is Billy, on my way."

It was thirty minutes past seven in the evening. The sky was dark and storm clouds were beginning to appear on the horizon. Pablo quietly entered the woods, unaware of what was about to happen later. He went deep into the woods, where not even the city noises could be heard. He got out of his car and started digging a grave. It was not an easy work and each minute felt like an hour. He buried Jeremy there.

Then he put the canvas that he had brought along with him on a stand and started painting – the trees, the night sky and the approaching storm clouds. The final touch was the gravestone peeping out through the bushes.

About thirty minutes later, when he had finished, he placed the canvas on the front seat very carefully. He then drove out of the woods, only to find a dozen police cars waiting for him outside.

"Put your hands up where I can see them," ordered David.

"Tim, what are you doing with the police?" asked a shocked Pablo.

"Game's over Pablo," said Antonio.

"Do you have any evidence against me young man?" asked Pablo, with a wicked smile.

"You were so busy painting that you didn't see us following you. We recorded everything you did. Burying Jeremy and painting the location. Also, you made a small mistake on your part – you forgot to hide the blood soaked clothes back at your house. What we have is enough to put you behind bars and I promise you it will be for lifetime," said David. "Billy, arrest him."

Realising that he has lost and there isn't a way out, Pablo pulled out his Glock 18 and aimed for the side of his own head. Before pulling the trigger, he said, "You will never understand what TRUE ART is."

Author Biography

11

Mala Bhattacharya

Mala Bhattacharya grew up with love for Literature in the beautiful Steel Township, Jamshedpur. Having completed her English Lit (Hons), she went on to complete her M.A. in English Literature. Shifting to Bombay post marriage, she entered the teaching arena as a teacher and HOD of English in various schools. Meanwhile, she obtained her B.ed degree with a First Class from Bombay University. Her principalship stint soon saw her helming

Sir J.J. Girls' High School, one of the oldest and prestigious institutions run by the benevolent and illustrious Jeejeebhoy family. Her second post - graduate degree in Education, M.A. (Ed) securing again a First Class ensured her smooth transition to the IGCSE (Cambridge) Boards, opted by 'National Education School'. At present after retirement, she continues, to tutor and mentor pupils online of different Indian as well as Cambridge Boards along with her other pursuits in Kolkata.

12

Madhurima Roychowdhury

Madhurima Roychowdhury hails from Kolkata, West Bengal, where she spent her formative years. Currently, she serves as an English teacher at Army Public School, ASC C & C in Bangalore. Apart from her dedication to education, Madhurima is a skilled Kathak dancer, passionately exploring various dance forms. She also has a profound appreciation for diverse cuisines. She believes in the therapeutic power of writing, viewing it as a means to heal deep emotional wounds. Poetry serves as her chosen medium for self-expression.

13

Debasri Mukherjee

I was born and grew up in a joint family in Kolkata, West Bengal, India. At that time everyone knew it as Calcutta.My schooling was at Loreto Convent. I went on to do my Bachelors and Masters in Human Physiology from the University of Calcutta. Then I did my Ph.D in Cardiovascular Physiology also from the Dept. of Physiology, University of Calcutta, under the supervision of Prof Debasish Bandyopadhyay.I did my post-doctoral research in immune-cell biology and proteomics from the

National Centre for Cell Science of the Dept. of Biotechnology, GOI, in Pune, Maharashtra, India. Then I joined Cactus Communications Pvt Ltd as a Scientific Writer.I am passionate about writing and have dabbled in multiple genres of fiction writing, from ghost stories to children's tales. Other than that, I enjoy swimming, traveling, and reading story books.My family comprises my parents, my aunt and uncle, my mother-in-law, my husband, and our black Labrador named Nemo (from Jules Verne's Captain Nemo. Not the fish).

14
Prakash Barai

Prakash Barai is an aspiring writer from the historical town of Krishnagar. He holds a Masters' degree in English from the University of Kalyani. Being a high school English teacher, he finds it fascinating to unfold the mystery of literature among the young buds. He has been passionate about writing since his college days, intending to see the world in a grain of sand and heaven in wild flowers. Many of his writings have been published in some national and international magazines. This is his second anthology as a co-author.

15

Dr Debosree Ghosh

Dr. Debosree Ghosh is an Assistant Professor in the Department of Physiology, Government General Degree College, Kharagpur II, West Bengal, India. Dr. Ghosh has been awarded Gold Medal by the University of Calcutta for holding 1st rank in M.Sc. in Human Physiology and received DST INSPIRE Fellowship in 2011 from the Ministry of Science, India, to pursue her Ph.D. in Physiology from the University of Calcutta. She has been awarded the Dr. D.N. Mullick Memorial Prize of the Physiological Society of India. She received a travel grant from the University of Calcutta for presenting her research work at the South Asian Association of Physiologists Conference, held in Colombo, Srilanka. She has been awarded a certificate of merit for the XXVI Training Programme on Science Communication and Media Practice held under the aegis of the Indian Science News Association. She has published more than 90 articles in peer-reviewed national and international journals. She has authored several book chapters in books published by national and international publishers. She has published more than 43 popular science articles in several newsletters. She has authored her first short story "An Unusual Winter Tale" in the anthology 'Winter Musings' published by Rhythmic Publishers. She is on the editorial board and serves as a reviewer in several national and international journals. She has delivered lectures at several national and international conferences in India and abroad.

16
Shreshtha Chowdhury

Shreshtha Chowdhury was born and raised in Kolkata. She did her post-graduation in English from Presidency University and is currently working as an independent scholar. She is deeply interested in adventure stories, histories, journals, novels and dark narratives. From being a cinephile herself, she loves to dive into the worlds of the cinematic universe. She had developed her zeal to explore the deep-seated origins and wide-reaching lessons of ancient myths with their themes, morals, customs and archetypes. She wishes for an enriching experience for all the readers who can immerse themselves and expand their imagination with extensive possibilities and realities.

17
Sanchita Chakraborty

Sanchita Chakraborty is a teacher at K. E. Carmel School, Suri. She holds a Master's degree in English and Culture Studies from The University of Burdwan. Passionate about exploring life through words, Sanchita inspires all to appreciate the shades of language and literature.

18
Sayan Mukherjee

Mr. Sayan Mukherjee has done his schooling from South Point High School. He has completed his Undergraduate Degree in B.Com(Honours) in Accounting and Finance from Netaji Nagar College(Evening) affiliated under The University of Calcutta. He loves to listen to music, especially rock and in his free time, he reads books of the detective genre. An art lover by nature, Sayan often paints. Sayan enjoys exploring hilly areas and Darjeeling is one of his favourite hill stations. Sayan loves to watch and play football and considers Lionel Messi to be his role model.